Original title:
The Chorus of the Canopy

Copyright © 2025 Creative Arts Management OÜ
All rights reserved.

Author: Thomas Sinclair
ISBN HARDBACK: 978-1-80567-306-4
ISBN PAPERBACK: 978-1-80567-605-8

Nocturne in the Nestled Nook

In the dark, the owls take flight,
Singing tunes that feel just right.
A squirrel's rant, a raccoon's cheer,
Dancing shadows, never fear.

A rabbit joins, with hops that gleam,
Whispers echo, a silly dream.
In cozy corners, laughter leaps,
As nighttime plays, and nature peeps.

The Soundtrack of Swaying Spruce

Beneath the boughs, the breezes howl,
Branches shake, like a jolly owl.
Chirps and croaks in rhythmic play,
Fast-paced tunes that lead astray.

A woodpecker's tap, a beat so spry,
Nuts and acorns roll, oh my!
Swaying trunks, the spruces dance,
Nature's soundtrack puts you in a trance.

Lyricism in the Leafy Realm

Leaves are rustling, crickets sing,
A chorus formed, oh what a fling!
The whispers joke, the bark has sass,
While nimble paws race on the grass.

A butterfly twirls, a dancer bold,
With graceful flutters, stories told.
In leafy nooks, strange rhythms blend,
Where laughter and nature often mend.

Reverie Under the Rustling Roof

Look up high, the stars pop in,
As critters gather, let the fun begin.
A raccoon wears a hat askew,
While fireflies play peek-a-boo.

The owlet giggles, a clumsy twist,
Swaying gently like a dance list.
Moonlit mischief fills the air,
Under this roof, joy beyond compare.

Interludes in the Ivy

Beneath the leaves where squirrels dance,
A fox tries hard to impress a chance.
With acorns flying, he takes a leap,
But lands right where the mosses creep.

The ivy whispers secrets loud,
While bees form up a buzzing crowd.
A worm in ties, he starts to groove,
And even snails can't help but move.

A chattering bird holds quite the show,
Telling tales of a rogue raccoon's woe.
The compost pile is a stage of glee,
As fungi sway, all wild and free.

So join the gang, don't be a bore,
In this leafy realm, there's laughter galore.
With every twist and every bend,
The ivy interludes never end.

Melodic Murmurs of the Meadow

The grasshoppers tune their tiny strings,
While daisies fashion crowns for kings.
A butterfly ballet flutters 'round,
As ants march proudly on the ground.

A toad croaks out an offbeat tune,
Claiming he's the meadow's moon.
With blooms that bob to the chuckle beat,
Each pulse of life is oh so sweet.

A meadowlark adds her silly squawk,
As beetles try to mimic her walk.
The clouds eavesdrop, puffed with pride,
While laughter spreads on the warm wind's tide.

So waltz along this vibrant spree,
Where sunshine shines with jubilee.
In harmonies of green and gold,
The meadow's stories dance, unfold.

An Anthem of Arborescence

Up in the branches, the parrots squawk,
Debating loudly on the best tree talk.
A wise old owl with glasses near,
Tries hard to learn their chatter here.

The woodpecker plays a thumping tune,
On a trunk that sways like a cartoon.
Each tap and click brings giggles out,
As raccoons join the pinecone shout.

Old leaves sway, they've seen it all,
From the smallest sprout to the tallest tall.
They chuckle softly, rustle with glee,
For nature's jesters, they all agree.

So gather 'round, both big and small,
In branches deep, there's room for all.
With every fruit and every jest,
In this tree, we dare to jest.

The Silent Sonatas of the Sun

Beneath the rays, the flowers giggle,
As sunflowers sway and dance, they wiggle.
A cheeky breeze with a playful sigh,
Tickles petals as butterflies fly by.

The sunbeams play peek-a-boo bright,
While shadows prance, a merry sight.
Each daffodil dons a golden grin,
Cheering for light to spin and spin.

A lizard lounges, basking wise,
While ants march forth in silly guise.
They party under the warm sun glow,
Believing they're stars in a grand show.

So tip your hat to the sunny fun,
Where laughter echoes, and all is spun.
In every flutter and every run,
The silent sonatas have just begun.

A Garden of Echoes

In a patch of green, where giggles grow,
Trees gossip softly, putting on a show.
Squirrels wear hats, they dance with flair,
Bunnies roll by, without a care.

The daisies laugh, their petals in bloom,
While crickets compose a night-time tune.
A chorus of leaves in a playful chat,
Join the fun, hear the woodland spat!

Crescendo of Canopies

Up in the branches, the owls are wise,
With spectacles perched, they secretly spy.
Raccoons play cards, with acorns as chips,
While turtles debate their best swimming flips.

Butterflies flutter, a colorful crew,
Playing hide-and-seek, just for a view.
The wind whispers secrets, with a cheeky grin,
Making everyone chuckle as the fun begins!

Murmurs of Moonlit Leaves

Under the moonlight, the branches sway,
With shadows that jiggle in a silly way.
Fireflies twinkle like tiny stars,
As raccoons sneak past with candy bars.

The night birds sing in a raspy tone,
Joining the laughter of the twilight zone.
While a goofy owl hoots, trying to impress,
The giggling leaves are a total mess!

Swaying Songs of the Summit

On the mountain peak, where the breezes tease,
The yodeling pines rise with elegant ease.
Chipmunks play pranks on the hikers below,
While giggles erupt from the streams that flow.

The clouds play tag in the blue, blue sky,
As the sun winks down, oh my, oh my!
Every leaf joins in, with a twist and a shout,
Nature's grand symphony, without a doubt!

Reverberations of the Rain

Raindrops dance on leaves so bright,
Each drop screams with pure delight.
Frogs croak tunes, a sticky band,
Worms wiggle to the beat, so grand.

Umbrellas flip, a comical sight,
Squirrels leap, full of fright.
Puddles splash, a squishy mess,
Nature's laughter, no need to stress.

Dialogues of the Dripline

Water drips, a rhythmic beat,
A clever snail takes a seat.
"Hey there, frog, what's your play?"
"Just waiting here for my cabriolet!"

Raindrops gossip, "Did you see?
A raccoon just tried to flee!"
Amidst the chatter, nature's crew,
Unfolds the tales, forever new.

Refrains of the Rainforest

Trees whisper secrets, leaves in cheer,
A lion's roar? It's just a deer.
Monkeys swing, a wild brigade,
While parrots squawk in bright parade.

Giggles echo from the brook,
As turtles ponder, "What's the hook?"
"Let's play hide and seek today!"
A game of stealth in green display.

Nature's Cadence Above

Clouds juggle rain like a clown,
While droplets play tag, up and down.
A penguin slips, all in good fun,
"Who knew rain could ruin a run?"

Bees buzz jokes, a zany crew,
As blossoms blush in vibrant hue.
Each petal swings to nature's song,
In this wacky world, we all belong.

Nature's Refrain

The squirrels debate their next big feat,
A nut heist planned, oh what a treat!
The birds tweet their songs, a catchy rhyme,
While ants march in sync, right on time.

A raccoon scrounges with style and flair,
Stealing snacks without a care!
The deer giggle, they're sly and spry,
As they leap away, oh my, oh my!

The sunbeams dance on the leaves above,
A playful whisper, a mockery of love.
While shadows stretch, they play peek-a-boo,
Nature's antics are never through!

So let's join this madcap, lively spree,
With critters and laughter; come, follow me!
For in this wild, where humor reigns,
It's the joy of life that forever remains.

Twilight Tones of the Timberline

As twilight wraps the trees in gold,
The owls gossip, their secrets told.
The rabbits race, in silly pursuit,
While fireflies flicker; what a hoot!

The raccoons don masks, so chic and neat,
Planning mischief, oh what a feat!
The frogs croak jokes, an evening show,
While crickets chirp, creating a glow.

Beneath the stars, the branches sway,
As foxes frolic in a grand ballet.
They tumble and roll with joyful screams,
Nature's antics fill the night with dreams.

So gather round as the night unfolds,
With every rustle, a tale retold.
In this world of whispers and delighted sighs,
Fun dances through the forest; it never dies!

Ephemeral Elegy of the Flora

In meadows bright, the flowers prance,
Each petal swirling, a vibrant dance.
The daisies giggle, the poppies sway,
In the breeze, it's a botanical ballet.

With bees in bowties, buzzing a tune,
They sip sweet nectar by the light of the moon.
The stems lean close, eavesdropping with glee,
Whispering jokes in floral esprit.

A dandelion puffs, its seeds take flight,
Like tiny wishes in the gentle night.
While clover huddles, sharing a joke,
As petals flutter, and laughing evokes.

In this transient space, the colors collide,
Creating hilarity, nature's joyride.
So join the bloom's tales of laughter and cheer,
For here in the garden, all woes disappear!

Dances in the Dappled Light

In sun-dappled glades, the shadows skip,
With playful feet that twirl and nip.
The mushrooms giggle, underfoot they hide,
While daisies grin, with petals spread wide.

The winds play pranks, tossing hats like kites,
While chipmunks race, oh what silly sights!
With bright eyes shining, the adventures flow,
As nature cracks jokes, in a whimsical show.

A hedgehog rolls in a dusty delight,
Making mud pies, oh what a sight!
The trees sway softly, a lullaby sound,
As laughter ripples through the earth all around.

So come for the fun, in the warm sunlight,
With nature as partner, what sheer delight!
In this dance of joy, let spirits take flight,
For every moment holds pure merry sprite!

Breath of the Biome

In the forest, squirrels dance,
Chasing acorns at a glance.
They trip and tumble, what a sight,
Stumbling under morning light.

Parrots squawk with glee and cheer,
Jokes about the lack of beer.
A monkey swings, a vine he grabs,
And lands right on a mob of jabs.

The trees above share tales so grand,
Of laughter lands and nuts unplanned.
Beneath the green, a ticklish breeze,
Whispers secrets among the leaves.

With every step, a critter shouts,
A beetle's laugh, with tiny bouts.
Nature's giggle fills the air,
In this wild space, we all can share.

Musings from the Mossy Floor

Here upon the mossy bed,
A worm confesses, 'I'm not fed!'
With every squirm, he tells his tale,
Of unripe fruits that seem to pale.

An ant nearby, in tiny pants,
Says, 'Dance with me, let's take a chance!'
But as he twirls, he slips and falls,
And bounces back, despite the brawls.

The mushrooms giggle, peeking out,
While fungi whisper with a pout.
'Why must the sun steal all the fame?'
Their caps are red, and it's a shame.

So here we linger, on the ground,
With critters singing, silly sounds.
Nature's floor, a comedic spree,
Reminding us to laugh with glee.

Wistful Wind through the Trees

The wind plays tricks with leaves so green,
They swirl and twist, as if they've seen.
A squirrel shouts, 'Catch me if you can!'
But who can catch a gusty plan?

Branches stretch with playful flair,
Whispering secrets, soft as air.
A chatty chipmunk, cheek stuffed tight,
Squeaks, 'Dinner's here! Oh, what a delight!'

The wind just giggles, darts away,
And splashes leaves in a playful spray.
The trees lean close, to joke and tease,
While grumpy boughs just aim to please.

In this wild theater of the green,
A stage of laughter, a leafy scene.
With every gust that tickles low,
It's the punchline that steals the show.

Dreams Among the Dirt

Down in the soil, the bugs convene,
With dreams of cakes, not just cuisine.
A caterpillar wants to bake,
But can't find arms, oh what a mistake!

Worms exchange tales of night and day,
'Wait, did you see that leaf ballet?'
They wiggle and giggle, underfoot,
Dreaming of roots and juicy fruit.

A snail named Fred plots a surprise,
For a party with glowworms as the prize.
He spins and twirls, his shell a blur,
While saying, 'Don't mind me, I just purr!'

Among the dirt, it's quite the scene,
With every laugh, the earth stays keen.
In this playground, quirky and spry,
The soil hums a happy sigh.

Verses Among the Verdancy

In the woods where squirrels play,
They wear tiny hats on the way.
Their acorns are gold, or so they say,
Ready for winter, not a moment's delay.

Trees dance like they're at some show,
With branches swaying to and fro.
A leaf drops down, a gentle blow,
Right in the nose of a gopher below.

The rabbits hop with comic grace,
Chasing shadows in a wild race.
One trips over a tuft, a blushing face,
Who knew they'd be such a clumsy case?

Beneath the boughs, the giggles spread,
As chipmunks gossip, their cheeks all red.
They barter seeds for tales instead,
In this lush green world where laughter's bred.

Ballads Beneath the Boughs

A singing frog starts up the jam,
With a croak that sounds like a jammed exam.
The turtles nod, 'tis quite the slam,
While a bird does the twist like a feathered ham.

The caterpillars rock and sway,
Riding leaves like a breezy ballet.
They'll inch along, make it their way,
And turn to butterflies in a bright display.

A wise old owl gives a chortle,
As the raccoons sneak near the portal.
With snacks they gather in a big huddle,
Planning pranks that are quite the ordeal.

The boughs above nod with delight,
As shadows dance in the fading light.
Nature's choir in silly sight,
Sings to the stars, oh what a night!

Songbirds in the Canopy

Songbirds chirp in perfect tune,
One insists he's the crooner of June.
He tries for a high note, oh what a swoon,
But sounds more like a howler, a cartooned moon.

A crow with style struts with flair,
Sporting a jacket, does he even care?
With every caw, he seems to declare,
That fashion in flight is a daring affair.

A parrot mimics the raccoon's call,
While a sparrow wonders if she's too small.
Together they form a chaotic thrall,
Making melodies among the tall.

And as day fades into twilight,
The owls join in, oh what a sight!
This band of oddballs is quite the bite,
In nature's stage, they're a peculiar delight.

Echoes of the Evergreen

In the evergreen, whispers collide,
As pine cones chuckle and giggle with pride.
One claims he's got the best inside,
While squirrels debate, their snacks all wide.

The wind plays tricks, blowing hats awry,
A raccoon stumbles, oh my, oh my!
"Is this a prank or just a sly,"
He mutters, while sparrows flutter and fly.

Beneath the needles, shadows skitter,
As nature's oddities gleefully glitter.
A toadstool takes a wild little critter,
Declaring, "It's me, the life of the litter!"

With giggles echoing through the trees,
The critters convene, they share a tease.
In the laughter of leaves, they find their ease,
In this uproarious world, all gathered to please.

Melodic Murmurs of the Multi-Colored Foliage

Leaves laugh and dance in breeze's sway,
Chasing bugs in a merry ballet.
Branches gossip about the clouds up high,
While squirrels plot to steal a pie.

Sunlight tickles every shade of green,
Frogs croak tunes, what a funny scene!
A squirrel wearing acorn on its head,
Makes all the birds giggle instead.

Raindrops tap like little drummers in fun,
While trees sway along, a musical run.
Bees hum jokes as they buzz and zoom,
Mirth fills the air, brightens the gloom.

Hilarious hums echo from below,
Each twig and leaf in a comical show.
Nature's laughter fills the vast expanse,
In this wacky green, they all prance.

The Pulse of Verdant Heights

Up in the trees where the breezes play,
A raccoon in sunglasses steals the day.
He struts around with his fluffy tail,
Claiming root beer, his new holy grail.

Vines twist and twirl, a clumsy dance,
While rabbits in bowties take a chance.
The air is thick with giggles and glee,
Nature's comedy, wild and free.

Parrots squawk silly jokes on a branch,
Telling tales in a vibrant prance.
The sun shines bright; all the colors cheer,
As shadows dance, bringing joy near.

With chirps of laughter, all creatures unite,
In a forest fiesta, what a delight!
From tiny ants to the tallest pine,
Every heartbeat laughs, oh so divine.

Whispers of the Woodland

Mushrooms grinning with faces so round,
Greet the wandering feet on the ground.
Pixies play in the shade of a tree,
While giggling fawns run wild and free.

A hedgehog spins in a playful roll,
While owls hoot jokes from their lofty hole.
With every rustle, a chuckle's shared,
Forest friends know how much they cared.

Dancing shadows and playful light,
Frogs in tuxedos jump with delight.
Breezes carry the whispers of fun,
In this merry place, joy has begun.

A chattering chain of joyful glee,
Nature's own stand-up, wild as can be.
Echoes of laughter weave through the trees,
In this woodland realm, all spirits please.

Echoes in the Emerald

In the emerald maze, mischief is sown,
Where every pine smells of ice cream cone.
Fireflies blink like tiny stage lights,
As beetles audition in dazzling tights.

Squirrels wear hats; acorns they toss,
With dance moves that would make one the boss.
Worms write rhymes as they wiggle below,
Making sure no one misses the show.

The brook gurgles jokes, bubbling with cheer,
Each splash a comedy, loud and clear.
A raccoon reclines, snack in each paw,
Shouting, "This is the life! Give me more raw!"

In this grove of giggles, joy is the king,
With roots that sway, and leaves that sing.
Life's a punchline in the tree-lined street,
In emerald echoes, everyone meets.

Amble Amidst the Abranches

Squirrels plot with acorn bombs,
While birds gossip of their charms.
The branches sway with silly songs,
And nature giggles, never wrong.

In leafy hats, the raccoons dance,
Pine cones twirl like a wacky prance.
A sneeze from pollen sets them off,
And laughter echoes like a scoff.

With every rustle, jokes abound,
As monkeys swing without a sound.
They mimic all, the king of farce,
In leafy realms, their spunk is sparse.

So come along, take time to roam,
In nature's jesting, you'll feel at home.
A frolic found in every tree,
Where laughter flows like honeybee.

Ancestral Echoes in the Arboretum

Grandpa tree tells tales of old,
Of sapling sneezes, brave and bold.
He chuckles at the leaves that fall,
A hat for squirrels, best of all.

A turtle slow, he can't quite keep,
With agile bunnies, skipping leaps.
He shares his wisdom, starts to rhyme,
While shadows dance to springtime's chime.

The whispering winds disrupt the peace,
As branches gossip, never cease.
A robin quips about the rain,
"Don't need a bath; it's all in vain!"

In every nook, a jest unfolds,
With laughter painted in the gold.
Among these giants, you may find,
A legacy of giggles, intertwined.

Forest Fantasia

Through the glades of glee we roam,
With mushrooms dancing, hearts at home.
The butterflies sport sunglasses sleek,
While grasshoppers perform their cheek.

In shadows loom the owls, all wise,
But even they can't hide their sighs.
For every twig that snaps apart,
Sprouts a new comic to the art.

Pine trees chuckle, old and spry,
Their bark's a mirror to the sky.
The forest floor, a laughter crowd,
As crickets chirp their jokes aloud.

So let's twirl with ferns so spry,
In nature's jest, we'll never die.
With each leaf's laugh, a new refrain,
Let joy explode like the autumn rain!

Sonnet of the Silent Woods

In silence wrapped, trees play their game,
Beneath their shade, we share the same.
A badger trips, oh what a sight,
He stumbles past, much to our delight.

The owl's wise wink, a quirky jest,
While chipmunks hide their nutty quest.
They giggle soft, behind their paws,
A sign of camaraderie, no flaws.

In burbling brooks, the fish take part,
And splash with glee, a watery art.
The forest's fun, in subtle ways,
Keeps shining bright through all our days.

So in these woods, where laughter reigns,
Release your cares, embrace the chains.
For every tree, a punchline waits,
In every glade, where joy translates.

Whispers Among the Leaves

In the breeze, the leaves do chat,
A squirrel's joke, a bird's chitchat.
Branches giggle, swaying round,
Nature's laughter, a joyful sound.

Mossy rocks play hide and seek,
While the ants march, tiny and sleek.
The sun peeks in, a playful tease,
Tickling branches, swaying with ease.

A raccoon grins with paws in the air,
As the butterfly twirls without a care.
Frogs in the bog croak out a tune,
Hoppers join in, dancing under the moon.

In this realm where joy prevails,
Every rustle tells funny tales.
So come and listen, join the spree,
In the foliage, wild and free.

Echoes of the Forest Floor

Beneath the trees, the creatures play,
Twirling leaves in a funny ballet.
Raccoons wear masks, oh what a sight,
While chipmunks giggle at the night.

The mushrooms chatter with cap and stem,
Silly jokes that make no sense to them.
Caterpillars waddle in bright, bold hues,
Wiggling on dance floors of morning dew.

Snakes slither by in a smooth, sly line,
While the shadows step to a rhythm divine.
Grasshoppers leap with a flick and a hop,
While the wise old owl takes a break from his shop.

Here every echo brings laughter loud,
A chorus of chuckles, nature's proud.
So tread lightly, join the funny thrill,
On the forest floor where whimsy is still.

Songs of the Sunlit Grove

Golden rays through branches peek,
Trees start humming, with tones unique.
Breezes laugh, twirling around,
While shadows dance on the ground.

Chirping crickets join the fun,
With beetles buzzing, they have begun.
Squirrels mimic puffs of air,
While dappled sunlight plays without a care.

The flowers sway, in colors bright,
As butterflies flutter, taking flight.
Bees buzz in rhythms, creating a hum,
Each note adds up, bringing the fun.

In the grove, the laughter stays,
Nature's music in joyful arrays.
So lend an ear, come join the tune,
In a sunny world, beneath the moon.

Harmony of the High Boughs

Up high where the branches stretch and sway,
A gathering of friends, hip-hip-hooray!
The crow cracks jokes, no one knows why,
While the diligent woodpecker gives it a try.

Chattering jays sing their loudest song,
As a pelican swoops, yet stays all wrong.
The owl rolls eyes as they flap about,
In their high boughs, there's no room for doubt.

Nuthatches giggle, swing from a thread,
While the pine cone's dropped, a funny dread.
The branches sway with each hearty laugh,
Creating wind's symphony, what a gaffe!

In this canopy where humor reigns,
Each leaf whispers rib-tickling gains.
So climb on up, join the frolicsome spree,
Where harmony blooms and giggles run free.

Timeless Tales of the Timber

In the woods where squirrels chat,
Bearded trees wear funny hats.
A raccoon juggles acorns bright,
While birds play tunes from morn till night.

A chipmunk's dance, a wobbly feat,
Stumbling 'round on tiny feet.
The branches laugh, they twist and sway,
As nature holds a cabaret.

The owls hoot jokes, oh what a scene,
As rabbits flash their best routines.
The shadows dance with every breeze,
Nature's jesters aim to please!

When moonlight glimmers through the leaves,
The timber's tales never deceive.
Whispered giggles in the dark,
A party hosted by a lark.

Reflections of the Foliage

The leaves gossip about the breeze,
With witty puns that aim to tease.
Frogs croak jokes, their rhymes miscast,
While bees buzz by, they fly so fast.

A beetle dons a tiny bow,
And struts about, putting on a show.
The flowers laugh, their petals twirl,
In this green world, life's a whirl.

The tales unfold of every prank,
The ponderous trunk gives one a flank.
Amidst the ferns, the spirit's keen,
Embracing each silly routine.

In reflecting pools where ripples dance,
The foliage shares its playful stance.
Oh, how they chuckle, through trees they hop,
Nature's stage, where giggles never stop.

The Treetop Symphony

Up high, the branch band starts to play,
With twinkling leaves that sway all day.
A squirrel strikes a chord on bark,
While drumming frogs make quite a spark.

The owls join in with hoots so loud,
Creating laughter from the crowd.
A raccoon claps, a tap on wood,
Unplanned mischief, life is good.

Hummingbird solos fill the air,
As flowers nod without a care.
The symphony's a fun delight,
Echoing through the starry night.

From treetop heights, the merriment sings,
Nature's humor on feathered wings.
With whispers soft, the forest cheered,
A concert hall, where none appeared!

A Sonnet Beneath the Sky

In open fields where daisies grin,
Grasshoppers leap, they wear a grin.
As butterflies launch a daring flight,
A wiggly worm dreams of a kite.

The sun peeks through with a twinkling eye,
While ants in suits march, oh so spry.
Each blade of grass sings in delight,
In nature's chaos, there's pure light.

Oh dandelions, you playful foes,
With wishes whispered, your magic glows.
The world's a stage for pranks and fun,
Beneath the sky, we're all as one.

So come and join this jolly spree,
Where laughter echoes, wild and free.
In every nook, a chuckle lies,
And joy abounds beneath the skies.

Symphony of the Leaves

In the trees, the leaves do sway,
A dance party every day.
Squirrels grooving, what a sight,
Their acorns flying, pure delight.

A rustling tune, a whisper low,
The breeze joins in, a breezy show.
Birds clap wings, they won't be shy,
Every branch a stage to try.

Chirping frogs in time, they croak,
With every twist, a leafy joke.
Sunlight's laughter through the green,
Nature's stage, a funny scene.

Leaves chuckle as the wind goes by,
"Don't lose your hats!" they call, oh my!
A symphony of giggles loud,
In the forest, we're all proud.

Murmurs of the Treescape

Whispers among the boughs would say,
The trees tell tales in a silly way.
A trunk in jabber, branches tease,
"Watch out below, I sneeze, I sneeze!"

A raccoon choir sings at night,
To the glow of fireflies, a sight!
Their tiny voices, soft and light,
Crickets join in, what pure delight!

The pinecone's drop, a thud and roll,
Playing catch, their joyful goal.
Old moss laughs with a gentle grin,
As branches twirl in a playful spin.

From roots to leaves, the humor flows,
Nature's laughter always grows.
In this treescape, we sing along,
Join the fun, where all belong!

Ballad of the Branches

Oh, the branches sway and bend,
In a goofy dance, around the bend.
They wave hello, they wave goodbye,
With leaves that twirl and try to fly.

Beneath the sky, a woodpecker taps,
To the beat of playful claps.
"Knock, knock!" comes a silly call,
"Who's there?" echoes through it all!

A butterfly flutters, what a show,
"Tag, you're it!" the flowers grow.
Each bud smiles, a blossom bright,
In this ballad, all takes flight.

Branches gossip, shake and sway,
"What's the rumor? What's today?"
Laughter echoes, in trees we trust,
With nature's joy, it's a must.

Lullabies of the Loft

In the lofted limbs of trees,
A choir hums in gentle breeze.
With giggles soft, as twilight falls,
The wood sings sweet, the night enthralls.

Crickets serenade the moon,
With rhythms that make shadows swoon.
"Count the stars!" they chirp with glee,
In this lullaby, oh so free.

Bats zoom by with a silly wink,
"Do you think we'll ever sink?"
While owls hoot their wise old tune,
Under the watch of silver moon.

So snuggle up in leafy beds,
With funny dreams and twisty heads.
Nature's lullabies, sweet and light,
Will cradle us through the night.

Nature's Ukulele

In the forest where squirrels dance,
A ukulele strums, it takes a chance.
Birds chirp their notes, a feathery jam,
While the raccoon beats drums; oh, what a slam!

The leaves sway along, in playful glee,
A chorus of laughter, just wait and see.
A frog joins in with a croaky refrain,
While the sun winks down, like it's all a game.

A turtle on a branch starts to sing,
His voice is slow, but oh, what a thing!
With a wink and a nod, others join in,
An orchestra forms, let the fun begin!

So grab your sticks, tap your feet to the beat,
Nature's jamming—not missing a beat.
Under the moon, all creatures unite,
Strumming their tunes till the morning light.

The Soundscape of Sun-Drenched Branches

Under the sun, the branches play,
A piper mouse pipes, what a wild display.
The chipmunks cheer, wearing tiny hats,
As the woodpecker taps, like a click-clacking cat.

Bees buzz a tune while flowers sway,
A conga line forms—who's leading today?
With a twist and a turn, the owls hoot loud,
Inviting all critters to join in the crowd.

Laughter erupts from the babbling brook,
As the fishes splash, writing their own book.
The sun tickles leaves, a ticklish delight,
And the grasshoppers hop and dance every night.

With branches that sway, the sky's our stage,
Nature's our world, we're all the same age.
So grab your friends, let the fun commence,
In this soundscape of joy, there's no need for sense!

Airborne Ballads in the Boughs

Up in the trees where the wild things sing,
A parrot takes lead, wearing bling-bling.
With melodies bright, they flap in delight,
Creating a ruckus, a musical flight.

A bat plays the piano, oh what a sight,
His wings flap keys in the soft moonlight.
While the owlets hoot, swaying side to side,
Joining the symphony, no one can hide.

A squirrel with style plays the guitar,
Strumming along while the rabbits hop far.
A maraca made from acorns shakes sweet,
As the nature band grooves to the woodland beat.

With verses that soar, these creatures are bold,
In boughs of the trees, their stories unfold.
So lift up your voice, let the laughter ignite,
In the airborne ballads, we dance through the night!

Treetop Tunes at Twilight

In twilight's glow, the branches swing,
A singing hedgehog starts to ring.
With a lullaby sweet, he rocks the night,
While glow-worms twinkle, what a sight!

The deer prance lightly, rhythm so neat,
With fireflies lighting, jazz on their feet.
As raccoons breakdance on starlit grass,
The beat of their moves makes the dark pass.

An owl dons glasses, becoming a sage,
He croons all the wisdom, page after page.
The crows form a choir, as funny as elves,
Singing of stories with giggles themselves.

So let's lift our heads, join the merry crew,
Under the moonlight, with nothing to rue.
With treetop tunes, let's sway and delight,
In a whimsical world, through the starry night!

Serenade of the Shimmering Glade

In a glade where the squirrels dance,
The rabbits join in a silly prance.
With acorns tossed like a game of catch,
They giggle and leap; oh, what a batch!

A turtle tried to join the fun,
But tripped on a root and began to run.
The frogs croaked loud, a comedic sound,
As the moonlight sparkled all around.

The fireflies decided to be the stars,
As they buzzed around like little cars.
A raccoon with a top hat struck a pose,
While a racquet-tailed bird sang all it knows.

At the end of the night, they shared a feast,
With berries, nuts, and a grinning beast.
Laughter echoed through trees so high,
In their shimmering glade, spirits flew high!

Melodies in the Mist

In morning fog, the critters play,
Dancing in a merry ballet.
The owls hoot out their best jokes,
As the mist giggles with the smokes.

The raccoons wear shirts, striped and bold,
Hosting a party that's never old.
The fog rolls in, a sneaky friend,
Whispering stories that never end.

A chattering bird squawks in delight,
As a squirrel attempts to take flight.
The branches sway with a chuckled tune,
While the sun peeks shyly, a playful boon.

Each leaf a note in nature's choir,
Strumming a rhythm that won't expire.
In friendly chaos, they find their bliss,
As they sway and swirl in the morning mist!

The Lullaby of the Lost Woods

In woods so lost, where whispers loom,
A beaver's tail begins to zoom.
With a splash and a laugh, it starts a tune,
To rouse the owls and dance with the moon.

A sleepy raccoon, with dreams on a log,
Woke up to find he's a dancing frog.
In a swirl of leaves, they break into song,
While the trees sway to the beat all night long.

The fox plays drums, with paws all a-flap,
While the badger spins in a humorous clap.
A parade of shadows, in giggles they roam,
Creating a chorus that feels like home.

As the stars twinkle in a game of peek,
The creatures laugh, playfully cheek to cheek.
In the lost woods, where fun never stops,
The lullabies echo, till slumber drops!

Voices of Veiled Branches

Under branches thick and bright,
Voices chirp in pure delight.
A squirrel with style, a vest of green,
Claims he's the coolest we've ever seen.

The snickering leaves share secrets low,
While buzzards compete in a silly show.
Each rustle and caw a comedic jest,
In this theater, they're all dressed best.

A lizard slides with a wink and grin,
Challenging friends in a topsy spin.
With every twirl, laughter's sound breaks,
Creating a rhythm like sweet pancakes.

As the sun dips low, the branches sway,
Filling the air with their joyful play.
In wondrous realms, where giggles blend,
The voices of branches never end!

Whistles of the Willows

Beneath the trees, the whispers play,
Where branches dance and children sway.
A squirrel spins a joke so sly,
While birds all giggle way up high.

Leaves rustle like a ticklish laugh,
Each gust of wind, a playful path.
The owls roll their eyes, so they say,
At the gossip of the leaves today.

Rabbits hop with silly grace,
Chasing shadows, a comical race.
Underneath the sky so blue,
Even the flowers smile for you.

In this green world, joy reigns supreme,
Nature's laughter is the best theme.
So join the fun, let's take a seat,
Beside the trees, life's truly sweet.

Hymns of the Herbaceous

In the patch where veggies grow and peek,
The zucchinis dance, oh so unique!
Carrots giggle beneath the ground,
While radishes boast of their round sound.

Parsley hums a whimsical tune,
Basil twirls beneath the moon.
Tomatoes blush with ripened cheer,
As peppers boast, "Get ready, dear!"

The cabbages roll in laughter loud,
As the peas form a giggling crowd.
Herbaceous friends, let's have a blast,
In the garden, fun is unsurpassed!

With a sprinkle of rain and a splash of Sun,
All together, we're bound to have fun!
So gather 'round, where the plants convene,
In this funny world of vibrant green.

Nature's Lyric in Green

In forests deep, where shadows play,
The critters sing in a jolly way.
A fox in socks flips through the leaves,
While rabbits chuckle and tease the bees.

The ferns sway like dancers on stage,
While mushrooms laugh, turning the page.
Worms hold a concert, wriggling tight,
In the rich soil, it's pure delight!

A chorus of crickets, a comical score,
As fireflies twinkle, wanting more.
Through the underbrush, chuckles abound,
In this symphony of joy, peace is found.

So take a walk in the lively scene,
Where nature's song is always keen.
With every step, let laughter flow,
In the living world, fun's the way to go!

Sonnet of the Swaying Boughs

Up in the trees, the branches tease,
As squirrels chatter with utmost ease.
A parrot cackles, a jester so bright,
While leaves sway gently, a lively sight.

The breeze tickles each bough with delight,
As shadows dance in the gleaming light.
A woodpecker drums with a raucous sound,
Turning the forest into a playground.

With every wobble and wiggle around,
The trunks join in, a laughter profound.
In this green amphitheater of fun,
The echoes of joy have just begun!

So come, let's mingle with nature's friends,
Where silliness sparkles, and laughter transcends.

Ballad of the Breezy Boughs

In the trees where giggles lie,
Branches sway, they dance and sigh.
Squirrels play their nutty tricks,
While birds debate on their favorite picks.

Leaves whisper tales of folly grand,
As acorns drop like a marching band.
A raccoon dons a leafy crown,
Proclaiming he's the king of the town.

Frogs serenade with croaks and leaps,
Their rhythmic waltz escapes the heaps.
Each twig a stage for antics wild,
Nature's laughter, ever beguiled.

So raise a toast to the leafy crew,
Who bring their joy in every view.
Underneath the shade, take a chance,
Join the trees in a whimsical dance.

Shouts of the Silvan Spirits

Among the trunks, the spirits shout,
Of silly games, there is no doubt.
An owl cracks jokes, while squirrels giggle,
As sunlight twinkles, they dance and wiggle.

Chipmunks rally for a nutty feast,
While nighttime critters, they play the beast.
A moth brings light with a flashy skirt,
As fireflies jest with a playful flirt.

The owls host nightly tongue-twisters,
While rabbits leap—oh, what a bluster!
Each creature joins in a merry spree,
Under starlit skies, oh the jubilee!

In the forest's depths, laughter rings,
A canvas of mirth that nature brings.
So come alive, hear the spirits cheer,
In the heart of the woods, there's nothing to fear.

Rhythms of the Rustling Foliage

Leaves prance lightly on nimble toes,
As the forest joins with laughter that flows.
Crickets keep beats with their chirpy song,
While shadows leap and twirl along.

A hedgehog scales a hill of grass,
As butterflies swirl in a colorful mass.
Dancing daisies in the morning light,
Invite all creatures to join the delight.

Breezes tease the branches above,
Whispering secrets of nature's love.
Ants march in rhythm, a tiny parade,
With leaves as banners, they won't be swayed.

Join in the fun, come sing with me,
In this merry land of jubilee.
Where every rustle plays a note,
Together we dance, let's gaily float.

Cadence of the Celestial Canopy

Beneath the stars, the moon shines bright,
As critters gather for a nightly fright.
A badger cracks jokes, the crowd erupts,
While owls roll eyes, as if they're unplumped.

The nightingale croons with a twist of glee,
Frogs join in—a wild jamboree.
Raccoons come dressed in masks and capes,
Imitating humans in crazy shapes.

The branches sway, a dance almost grand,
While shadows waltz upon the land.
Every leaf a prop, every branch a stage,
Nature's comedy, free of cage.

So laugh along to the woodland song,
Where everyone feels they truly belong.
In the rich embrace of the rustling bough,
Let's celebrate this moment—here and now.

Rhythms of the Rainforest

In the jungle, the monkeys swing,
They boast of their acrobatic flair.
While parrots squawk, doing their thing,
A toucan takes charge of the air.

Sloths hang tight in a sleepy embrace,
Dreaming of climbing up high.
While ants on parade move with pace,
To a tune no one can deny.

Frogs provide the finest of beats,
Ribbiting in perfect sync.
As lizards join, tapping their feet,
Who knew they're such great drink-clink?

The liverwort dances, bouncing around,
While ferns sway with graceful flair.
This is where tight-knit friends are found,
And laughter is caught in the air.

Cadence of the Canopy

Squirrels chatter about who's the best,
Debating who's stealing the show.
With nutty plans put to the test,
As the breeze gives a playful blow.

A parrot dons a flamboyant hat,
While a snake tries on a cool disguise.
The toucan, proud, puffs out like that,
With all of his colorful cries.

Caterpillars twirl like they're stars,
In a dance that's purely absurd.
While a beetle brags about his new car,
"This ride is simply unheard!"

A rhythm so silly, it sparks delight,
Through cupped leaves, the laughter resounds.
Nature's antics from morning till night,
In a symphony where joy abounds.

Melodies in the Moss

On a log, a frog claims the stage,
Croaking with gusto, quite proud.
While the rest of the critters engage,
In a dance that wouldn't be loud.

Moss springing forth like dancers in bloom,
While mushrooms chime in with a shout.
The scent of wet earth fills the room,
As the forest plays hard to pout.

Termites tap dance with their tiny feet,
Shaking off dirt, no time to waste.
Raccoons join in to steal the beat,
As they munch on a sweet little taste.

With shadows stretching as stories unfold,
Laughter echoes through branches near.
In the undergrowth, tales told and bold,
Resound in a whimsical cheer.

Chorus of the Highboughs

Up high, the branches sway and grin,
As bees buzz around with delight.
A squirrel pipes up, "Who let you in?"
And the chatter begins in flight.

Owl cracks jokes, he's the wise old sage,
While the bats hang upside-down and cackle.
They ponder life's silliest stage,
And sometimes, they even crackle.

Vines twist in rhythm, a twist of fun,
Hummingbirds visit, a blur of cheer.
With petals and laughter, they come undone,
Bringing joy for all to hear.

In this realm, where mischief ensues,
Every leaf joins the jubilant quip.
Nature's expressiveness in splendid hues,
And humor takes each playful trip.

Rhapsody of the Roots

In the dance of the dirt, they waltz with glee,
A tangle of tubers, as goofy as can be.
With whispers of wisdom from deep underground,
They plot silly games where the squirrels abound.

The worms join in, wriggling left and right,
Beneath the old oak, what a goofy sight!
They laugh at the critters that stomp on their toes,
"Don't mind us, we're just up for some rooty shows!"

A bulb with a joke that always gets a grin,
Roots trading puns while the mushrooms spin.
"Hey, what did the tree say to its mate?
Stop leafing me alone, it's just too late!"

So if you hear laughter from beneath your feet,
Just know that the roots are having a treat.
In the rhapsody down where the soil groans,
A comedy's brewing in nature's own tones.

Chants of the Cedar

The cedars are singing, oh what a sound,
With the birdies as backup, their voices abound.
"Hey, I'm a tree, just reaching for sky,
But look at my branches, they wave, oh my!"

They chuckle a tune with a lumberjack's flair,
Fluffy squirrels tumble like they don't have a care.
"Who needs a haircut? Just let me grow wild!
I'll take the whole forest, come join this child!"

Dropping acorns like raindrops, with a mischievous grin,
A game of catch with the pinecones begins.
"Catch this one, and I'll throw you a branch,
Let's see if you're quick, or if you're a ranch!"

The chants fill the woods, a symphonic delight,
With cedar rhythms dancing well into the night.
In laughter, they linger, and life goes on,
Nature's own chorus, where joy is not gone.

Soliloquy of the Shadows

Underneath the green, where shadows play,
A tree's busy thinking in a quirky way.
"Why do they call me the shade-maker here?
All I do is stand, but they treat me like beer!"

With critters beneath doing their best charade,
The leaves laugh together, it's quite the parade!
"Hey, I'm a fan – one moment in breeze,
Chill out, little critters, I aim to please!"

The shadows keep teasing the squirrels and crows,
"Catch me if you can!" as the funny wind blows.
A dance of illusions, all flickers and fun,
Who knew shadows could be so clever and spun?

Whispers and giggles in the soft summer hue,
They weave silly tales in the light breaking through.
An unending jest, as the sun sinks low,
In the theater of twilight, where laughter can grow.

An Ode to the Overstory

High up in the branches where big dreams soar,
There's laughter and chatter, a vine-covered floor.
"Here's a secret, keep it — I'm more than a tree,
I'm a stand-up comic, just look at me!"

The forest is thriving with jokes oh so witty,
While the owls roll their eyes, saying, "Ain't that pretty!"

Bugs buzz in chorus, their humor the same,
"Why did the acorn join in on the game?"

"To find its true roots! What a humorous quest!
You should see our tree house, we're building a nest!"
The canopy chuckles, as branches entwine,
In a show of the greenery, they perfectly shine.

An ode to the tales that sprout from each leaf,
In the world up above where laughter's the chief.
Nature's own joke book, with pages so vast,
Every twist and turn, a giggle built to last.

Chants Across the Canopy

Leaves above, they chatter, oh so loud,
Squirrels dance, joining in, acting proud.
Birds on branches, with melodies so bright,
Crafting tunes from dawn till fading light.

A raccoon sings, tail swaying to the beat,
While ants march in, tapping tiny feet.
Everyone's invited to this merry show,
Nature's laugh, it echoes high and low.

Laughter bounces off each trunk and tree,
While frogs croak, quite the comedic spree.
The wind joins in, with a playful breeze,
Whispering secrets through the rustling leaves.

This forest fest is never done,
With critters vibing, oh what fun!
Nature's concert, wild and free,
In this leafy realm, we all agree!

Nature's Whisper

Amidst the trees, the voices rise,
A playful breeze, under sunny skies.
Crickets chirp, their own little tune,
While raccoons play, dancing around the moon.

A woodpecker knocks, like a drummer's stick,
Singing along with a squirrel's quick flick.
The flowers giggle, swaying to the sound,
Every corner of the woods, merriment found.

Frogs croak in harmony, what a sight,
As bees buzz by, their buzzes light.
The bushes rustle, gossiping trees,
Sharing stories with the fluttering leaves.

Beneath the sun, nature's voice is clear,
With hidden laughter, we all can hear.
Join the fun, let your spirit soar,
In this wild world, there's always more!

Symphony in the Shade

Here in the shade, there's a wild crew,
Giggling streams and dancing dew.
Beetles tap dance, a shiny parade,
In this leafy space, laughter's displayed.

A parrot squawks, quite an amusing loud,
Juggling bright fruits, feeling so proud.
While the owls hoot their own funky song,
In this verdant spot, where all belong.

Occasional rustles, a mystery's tease,
What's under that leaf? A giggle or sneeze?
The sun peeks through, with a golden glance,
And all nature starts its funniest dance.

So grab your hat, and join the throng,
In this leafy world, where we all belong.
Every critter plays a joyful part,
A merry symphony, straight from the heart!

Secret Songs of the Shrubbery

In the shrubbery, secrets unfurl,
As tiny critters around me twirl.
The bushes hum tunes, so sweet and rare,
While chubby hedgehogs roll without a care.

A fox sneezes, it echoes around,
While snails take their time, not making a sound.
The bunnies hop, in rhythm they leap,
Their giggles resound, in the shadows they creep.

A caterpillar sings, 'I'll soon be a star!',
While ladybugs chuckle, cruising afar.
Crickets join in with a clattering cheer,
In this green haven, good vibes are near.

So let us wander where the laughter sprouts,
Among the leaves, we'll chase away doubts.
Nature's whimsy is ours to explore,
In a world of giggles, there's always more!

Rhapsody Among the Roots

Squirrels dance with acorn hats,
Where tree frogs croak and doormat chats.
The branches giggle, leaves take flight,
As shadows stretch and bask in light.

A woodpecker taps like a drummer bold,
While ants parade with treasures of gold.
The breeze tells tales of twigs gone wrong,
In this lively place where all belong.

Beneath the ferns, a turtle grins,
Wearing a smile, it never thins.
With every wiggle, there's laughter song,
In the roots where funny things belong.

When twilight comes, the fireflies blink,
They tease the dusk, stars start to wink.
In the rapture of whispers and delight,
Nature's shenanigans fill the night.

Echoing Through the Evergreen

Pine cones tumble like playful jest,
While owls debate who'll get the best nest.
The eagles chuckle as they soar so high,
And raccoons try their hand at a pie.

The squirrels argue about acorn theft,
With nuts thrown back, there's new 'branch' left.
The bushes shake in silent giggle,
As rabbits tease and wiggle, wiggle.

Moose strut past, with antlers so grand,
They strike a pose; it's all quite planned.
While beavers march with sticks aligned,
In a band of buddies, all intertwined.

Laughter floats on a breeze so sweet,
Where every animal meets and greets.
In evergreen realms, with humor so fine,
Nature's comedy is quite divine.

The Swaying Symphony

Leaves sway gently, dance to the beat,
Of windy whispers that tickle their feet.
A hedgehog jives, its spines all a-quake,
While frogs on lilypads leap and shake.

The crows create a raucous choir,
While chipmunks join, their voices inspire.
A snake with rhythm, all slithery and slick,
Looks on in envy, wishing for a trick.

The flutter of wings, a comical sight,
As butterflies tumble in dizzy delight.
The roots all chuckle, a grounding cheer,
As nature rocks out, year after year.

In shady recesses, laughter ignites,
With every misstep bringing more delights.
The swaying symphony makes hearts sing,
In playful chaos, all creatures swing.

Harmonies in the Hidden Realm

In the shade where whispers float,
A toad croaks softly, wearing a coat.
With mischief twinkling in its eye,
A breath of laughter sweeps by.

Bushes rustle with secrets to share,
A fox scuffles up, striking a flair.
The bees hum tunes as they flit and dart,
Painting the air with nature's art.

A porcupine prances, poky and proud,
While mice in jackets squeak loud.
The earthworms wiggle, taking their place,
In this concert of joy, there's no trace of haste.

As day turns to night, the critters unite,
They sway to melodies that feel just right.
In this hidden realm where fun's the theme,
Nature's harmonies form a laughter stream.

Reflections in the Rustling

In the leaves, a squirrel sings,
With acorns tucked beneath his wings.
He tries to dance on branches high,
But trips on twigs and flops nearby.

A wise old owl wears glasses tight,
To read the forest's gossip right.
He winks at trees and hoots with glee,
While sparrows giggle, 'Look at he!'

The breeze just laughs, a playful tease,
As branches bow like dancing knees.
And all the creatures in their play,
Invite the sun to join and sway.

So every rustle holds a cheer,
In nature's jest, so bright and clear.
With all the whimsy that it brings,
Life's full of laughter and of things.

Verses of the Vines

Twisting like a tangled rhyme,
Grapevines giggle, keeping time.
They weave a tale of wine and cheer,
While playful critters lend an ear.

A frog hops in, a bard so bold,
With stories of the pond retold.
He croaks a tune, off-key but bright,
As spiders dance, oh what a sight!

The sun sneezes through the leafy green,
Tickling all in the place between.
A beetle drums on bark with flair,
While bees hum tunes, a buzzing air.

Each vine a line of laughter spun,
Entwined in jest beneath the sun.
With every twist, a tale to spare,
In nature's party, none compare!

Poetry of the Pine

Pine trees rattling in the breeze,
Whispers spread like giggles, please!
Their needles drip with stories old,
Of squirrels' pranks and joys untold.

A pine cone slips, takes quite a fall,
Landing on the back of a brawl.
Two chipmunks argue, who gets the prize,
While nearby, a crow just rolls its eyes.

The needles chuckle, swaying low,
While squirrels plan their heist in tow.
With acorns launched like cannonballs,
They laugh and shout through nature's halls.

In every ring, a joke is spun,
The pines make merry, life's so fun.
With every rustle, joy's set free,
In the tall tales of each pine tree.

Treetop Testaments

In treetops high, the breezes chat,
They swap their tales like this and that.
A blue jay boasts, 'I've got the flair!'
While, below, a raccoon just stares.

A daring squirrel with shades of cool,
Plays hide and seek and breaks the rule.
He scampers up, then down he zooms,
While laughing leaves whisper in blooms.

Rooted trees shake their branches free,
And shout aloud, 'Come laugh with me!'
In this canopy of playful spins,
Where every day, adventure wins.

Beneath the sky, so bright and vast,
Each creature's jest brings joy to last.
In nature's theater, what a show,
Treetop tales make spirits glow!

Aria of the Arbor

In branches high, the squirrels dance,
They twirl and leap, it's quite the prance.
The owls hoot jokes, both wise and bright,
While fluttering leaves join in the flight.

A woodpecker taps a lively beat,
As ants march high on tiny feet.
The sunbeams giggle, a warm embrace,
While shadows play a playful chase.

Harmonies of the Hidden

In hidden nooks, the critters sing,
With all their hearts, as if on a swing.
The raccoon jokes with a cheeky grin,
While ladybugs hide and tease within.

Frogs croak tunes from the mossy bog,
Beneath the stars, they leap and jog.
The fireflies blink in a sparkling show,
Whilst a sleepy hedgehog steals the glow.

Lullabies of the Leafy

A gentle breeze whispers sweet rhymes,
As crickets chime with their nighttime chimes.
The branches sway, a lullaby tune,
While the moon chuckles, a silly cartoon.

The owlets giggle in their snug nests,
Feeling cozy, they take their rests.
With twinkling stars above so bright,
They snooze away in pure delight.

Voices of the Aerie

In the high nest, the young birds squawk,
They tumble around, a feathery shock.
A parent swoops with snacks galore,
And all the chicks cheer, "More! More! More!"

Breezes tease with a playful shove,
As winged pirates chase and shove.
The sky above, a canvas wide,
Where silly dreams take daring pride.

Hymn of the Hoary Canopies

Up in the trees, where squirrels dare,
They hold debates in the fresh, cool air.
With acorns flying and laughter loud,
They tease the owls, so wise and proud.

Branches sway as birds will prance,
While ants below perform a dance.
A chipmunk juggles pine cones with glee,
Declaring himself the king, you see!

In every nook, the laughter rings,
Where even the insects try to sing.
The leaves chuckle softly in the breeze,
And whisper secrets to the teasing trees.

As night draws near, the moon will glow,
The forest critters put on a show.
With fireflies flickering bright and bold,
The tales of the canopy are told.

Harmony of the Hills

In the hills where the wild things play,
A goat on a rock sings every day.
With a sock on his horn, he struts with pride,
While the sheep roll eyes, trying to hide.

A raccoon in shades claims he's the star,
Sipping dew drops like he's at a bar.
The rabbits giggle in their fuzzy coats,
As the clever fox steals his merry notes.

The frogs croak hymns in their muddy choir,
While butterflies dance, lifting higher and higher.
The ants march by in a disciplined line,
While snails peek out for a glimpse at the divine.

Even the winds join the playful sound,
Tickling leaves as they dance around.
The hills erupt in a giggling spree,
A symphony of nature, wild and free.

Whispers in the Wildwood

In the wildwood, where shadows play,
The critters plot on a sunny day.
With a mischievous grin, the raccoon leads,
While the hedgehogs toil, planting weeds.

A parrot squawks jokes from high above,
While sloths hang out, sharing their love.
The beavers build, with a splash and a thud,
As the frogs leap in for a friendly mud.

Squirrels trade stories of winter's woe,
As foxes roll over in sun's warm glow.
Each branch holds laughter, each leaf a grin,
As nature hums with a cheeky spin.

At dusk, the hoot of the owl resounds,
Bringing about the magical sounds.
As night falls gently, the stars start to peep,
In the wildwood whispers, secrets to keep.

Lullaby of the Leafscape

In the leafscape, where dreams take flight,
A chubby raccoon steals cookies at night.
He nibbles and grins, with crumbs on his fur,
As the fireflies flash, they giggle and chirp.

A sleepy old owl sings to the moon,
While the hedgehogs snore to a soft, sweet tune.
The bunnies ballet in the shimmering light,
With petals for tutus, laughter takes flight.

The trees sway gently with stories to share,
Of dove duels and windy hair.
The sun's warm glow playfully dips,
A symphony lingers on twinkling lips.

As the stars gather, the night feels alive,
With shimmering tales that always survive.
In the leafscape, where joy never stops,
Nature's lullaby twirls and hops.

The Overture of Overhead

Squirrels debate on acorn stocks,
While pigeons dub their knock-knock knocks.
Branches sway like a dance-off scene,
As the sun glows bright with a golden sheen.

Frogs croak tunes in a jazzy spree,
Next up, a woodpecker's symphony.
Breezes tickle leaves with gentle hums,
Underneath, the goofy groundhog drums.

Mice play chess on a mossy board,
While owls provide a wise accord.
The clever raccoons roll on the floor,
Saying, "Who ordered pizza at the door?"

Nature's band strikes a comical pose,
With each note, the laughter grows.
Tune in to the chaos so bright and loud,
In this treetop circus, we're all quite proud.

Chants of the Whispering Pines

Whispering winds share secrets near,
While pinecones dance without a fear.
A fox makes jokes about tree size,
While the rabbits giggle 'til they cry.

Beneath the needles, shadows play,
As chipmunks show off in the fray.
The twirl of a squirrel in fuzzy socks,
Keeps the atmosphere filled with talks.

Pine trees tease with their sticky sap,
As jays dive in for a midair clap.
Grumpy old owls hoot with flair,
In their wild ruffles, they look quite rare.

Echoes of laughter swirl around,
In this forest, joy's always found.
So join the chant in the cool pine glade,
For every giggle, a dance parade!

Anthems of the Ancient Oaks

Under the branches, tales unfold,
Where acorns drop like stories told.
Squirrels shout, "It's a nutty tale!"
As deer plot pranks, they'll never fail.

The oaks stand tall with a knowing grin,
Laughing at mischief, where to begin?
Epic tales of the wind and bark,
Join the fun in this woodland park.

Crickets chirp with a rhythmic twist,
While raccoons feast on a pie they missed.
A wise old owl, with a bellyache,
Says, "Who knew that snacks could be this fake?"

The night drapes down with a blanket thick,
And all gather 'round for a ghostly trick.
With echoes of fun in the rustling leaves,
The ancient oaks wear laughter like sleeves.

The Symphony of Shadows

In the dusk, where shadows play,
Crickets serenade the end of day.
Kittens chase their own tails tight,
As fireflies twinkle, lighting the night.

In the alleys of dusk's soft shade,
Bunnies hop in a silly parade.
Their ears flopping to the rhythm sweet,
While jays sing loudly with dainty feet.

The moon peeks in with a cheesy grin,
As owls spin tales that entice a grin.
What's that sound? A disco fox!
Leading the night in silly paradox.

In twilight, chaos reigns so grand,
Each critter joined a merry band.
A symphony bright in the fading light,
Bringing joy 'til dawn takes flight.

Harmonies in the Hollow

In the trees, a squirrel sings,
With acorn hats and lively flings.
A rabbit joins, a tap-tap-tap,
While birds groove on, in leafy flap.

Beneath the boughs, a worm does dance,
In muddy boots, he takes a chance.
With silly moves, he wriggles around,
While the shy moles peek from underground.

The wind plays flute, the leaves all cheer,
As the party cranks up with every cheer.
Frogs croak choruses, so off-beat,
As ants march in with tiny, quick feet.

In nature's band, no one's aloof,
They jive and giggle, that's the proof.
Each creature hums, no time to pout,
In this hollow, it's all about!

Serenade of the Sunlight

Bees buzzing tunes, in golden rays,
While flowers sway, in happy displays.
A cat takes a stretch, sunbeam delight,
A lazy grin, oh what a sight!

The sun above, a giant ball,
Makes shadows dance, oh what a haul!
A lizard slides, to join the beat,
With a tail-twist that can't be beat.

Frolicking beams, they weave and spin,
As tiny ants sip lemonade with a grin.
Squirrels juggle nuts with flair,
As laughter echoes through the air.

Oh, what a floor, this sunny stage,
With every creature, out of their cage.
In the light, they shimmy and shine,
In this bright world, everything's fine!

Voices of the Verdant

A porcupine wails, part-time star,
With needle-sharp notes that travel far.
The possum plays tambourine,
While the chipmunk busts a silly routine.

The ferns do sway, lost in the sound,
As raccoons twirl round and round.
Each flower shimmies, a droplet's clink,
In the green, they all dance and wink.

Crickets strum their tiny guitars,
While crows form a band beneath the stars.
A bear breaks it down, with a little jig,
The forest chuckles at his big pig!

Through tangled vines, the giggles flow,
It's a happy crew, as they steal the show.
In this world, where laughter's abound,
Voices of nature, joyous, profound!

Songs of the Sylvan

In the thicket, a fox takes lead,
With a wink and a grin, he plants the seed.
A chorus of crickets, a shimmery night,
As the fireflies blink in playful delight.

Trees sway gently, wearing their crowns,
Cheeky raccoons in borrowed gowns.
Hooting owls act as the DJ,
Spinning tales till the break of day!

With a thump and a bump, the hedgehog rolls,
In a tumble of laughter, his antics console.
A band of rabbits, with feet all a-tap,
Join the fun in this woodland frap.

As the dusk draws near, the party stays,
With animal antics and silly craze.
In this sylvan world, they burst out in song,
In the heart of the woods, where all belong!

Rhythmic Revelations Overhead

In the trees, the squirrels dance,
With acorns flying, what a chance!
A parrot mimics all our cries,
While monkeys swing beneath the skies.

The wind whistles a playful tune,
As branches sway beneath the moon.
A raccoon juggles berries bright,
And fireflies join in the night.

A playful breeze begins to tease,
While owls hoot jokes with expert ease.
The leaves laugh softly, rustle, squeal,
In this woodsy waltz we can all feel.

So come and join this woodland show,
Where nature's laughter steals the glow.
With every rustle, chirp, and cheer,
The canopy's humor draws us near.

Breathless Ballad of the Breeze

Oh, listen to the playful gust,
That puffs up cheeks and stirs the dust.
A chipmunk sports a tiny hat,
While trying to chase down a fat cat.

The dandelions spin about,
As butterflies join in, no doubt.
A breeze tickles the sleeping leaves,
Whispering laughter as it weaves.

Each flutter brings a silly sight,
As nature's critters take to flight.
With giggles floating in the air,
The trees wink softly, debonair.

So come, enjoy this breeze-filled spree,
Where nature's humor sets us free.
In every gust and gentle sway,
A joyous tune to greet the day.

www.ingramcontent.com/pod-product-compliance
Lightning Source LLC
Chambersburg PA
CBHW072149200426
43209CB00051B/970